Introducing CHOPIN

ROLAND VERNON

Chelsea House Publishers
Philadelphia

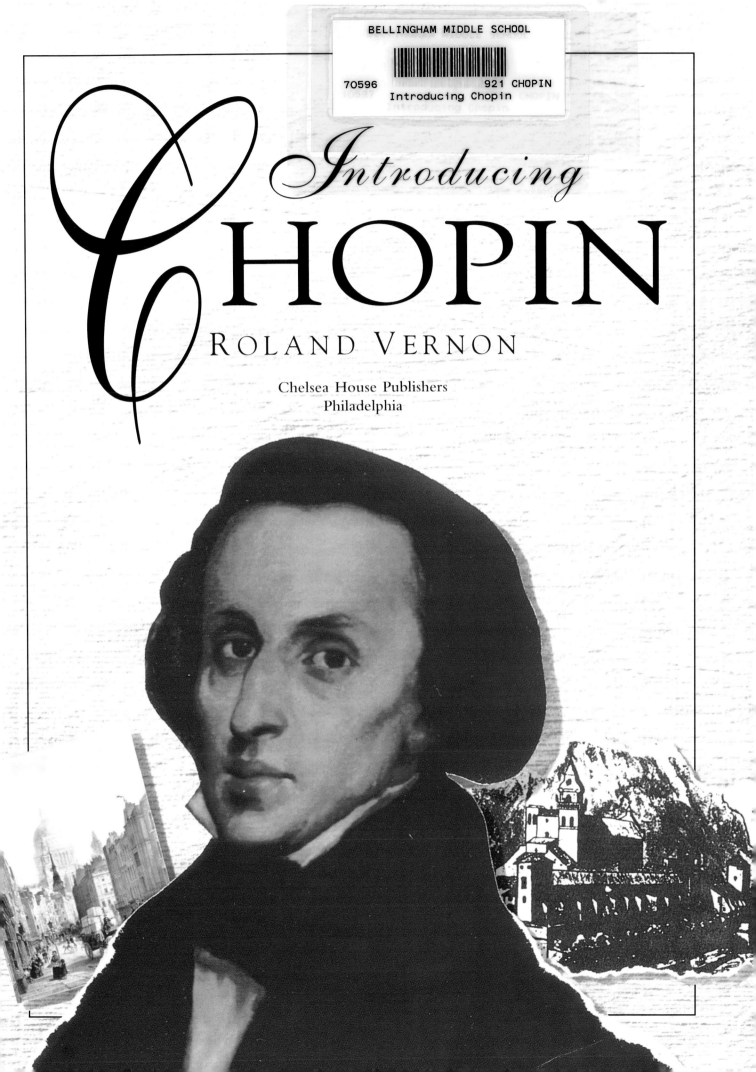

First published in hardback edition in 2001
by Chelsea House Publishers, a subsidiary of
Haights Cross Communications. All rights reserved.
Printed and bound in China.

First published in the UK in 1996 by
Belitha Press Limited, London House,
Great Eastern Wharf, Parkgate Road,
London SW11 4NQ, England

Text copyright © Roland Vernon 1996
Illustrators copyright © Ian Andrew 1996

Editors: Christine Hatt and Claire Edwards
Designer: Wilson Design Associates
Picture Researcher: Diana Morris

First printing
1 3 5 7 9 8 6 4 2

The Chelsea House World Wide Web address is
http://www.chelseahouse.com

Library of Congress Cataloging-in-Publication Data applied for.

ISBN: 0-7190-6039-X

Picture acknowledgments:
AKG London: front cover, back cover t, 12b, 14t, 17t, 24b, 27t, 29b.
Apsley House, London/Bridgeman Art Library: 7t. Barnaby's Picture Library:
6t. Trustees of the British Library: 16t. Chateau de Malmaison/Lauros-
Giraudon/Bridgeman Art Library: 7b. Fryderyk Chopin Society: 8b, 28.
Conservatory of St. Peters, Naples/Giraudon/Bridgeman Art Library: 9t.
E.T. Archive: 6c, 6b, 14b, 18t. Mary Evans Picture Library: 25b. Guildhall
Library, London/Bridgeman Art Library: 26t. Robert Harding Picture Library:
19t, 29t. Historishces Museen, Vienna/Bridgeman Art Library: 13t. Hulton
Deutsch Collection: 15t, 16b. Leipzig Museum/AKG London: 11. Louvre,
Paris/Giraudon/Bridgemann Art Gallery: 24t. Mansell Collection: 22t. Musée
National, Versailles/AKG London: 22b. Musée D'Orsay/Giraudon/Bridgeman
Art Library: 23b. Bildatchiv der Osterreicheschen Nationalbibliothek, Vienna:
10. Private Collection/Bridgeman Art Library: 9b. Private Collection/
Index/Bridgeman Art Library: 20t. Staatliche Museen zu Berlin, PK
Nationalgalerie: 13b. Uffizi Gallery, Florence/ET Archive: 23t.
Victoria & Albert Museum, London/Bridgeman Art Library: back cover b, 26b.

CONTENTS

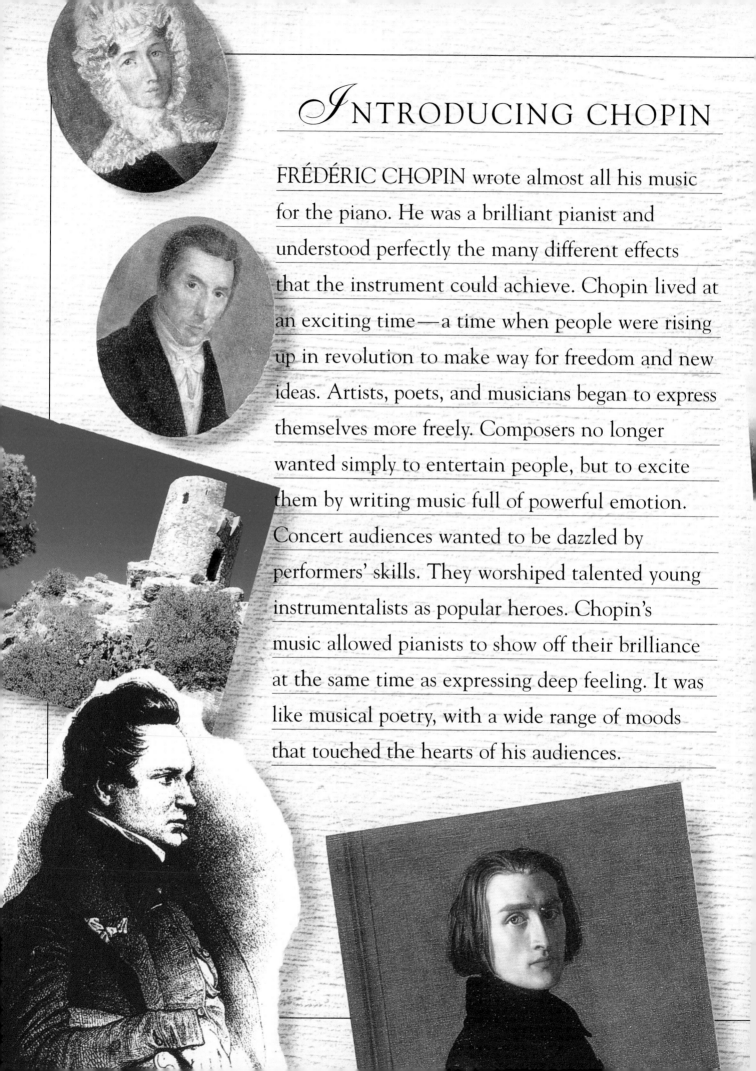

INTRODUCING CHOPIN

FRÉDÉRIC CHOPIN wrote almost all his music for the piano. He was a brilliant pianist and understood perfectly the many different effects that the instrument could achieve. Chopin lived at an exciting time—a time when people were rising up in revolution to make way for freedom and new ideas. Artists, poets, and musicians began to express themselves more freely. Composers no longer wanted simply to entertain people, but to excite them by writing music full of powerful emotion. Concert audiences wanted to be dazzled by performers' skills. They worshiped talented young instrumentalists as popular heroes. Chopin's music allowed pianists to show off their brilliance at the same time as expressing deep feeling. It was like musical poetry, with a wide range of moods that touched the hearts of his audiences.

The house in Zelazowa Wola where Frédéric Chopin was born in 1810. By October of the same year, the family had moved to Warsaw.

Nicholas and Justyna Chopin were married in 1806. They were devoted parents, who supported Frédéric's passion for music.

A HAPPY FAMILY

Frédéric Chopin was born on March 1, 1810, in a small Polish village called Zelazowa Wola. His father, Nicholas, came from a French farming family, but traveled to Poland at the age of 16. After working in a tobacco factory, Nicholas fought bravely for Poland against the Russians, then became a tutor to children of the **aristocracy**. He and his wife, Justyna, had four children of their own—Louise, Frédéric, Isabella, and Emilia. They were a close and happy family. Soon after Frédéric's birth, they moved to Warsaw, where Nicholas became French teacher at the city's **Lyceum**.

Frédéric was a dreamy, poetic, and very sensitive child. But he had a great sense of fun and was particularly clever at imitating people's voices and actions. He also entertained his friends and family by drawing humorous **caricatures**. His childhood in Poland was the happiest time of his life, darkened only by the tragic death of his youngest sister, Emilia, from **consumption** in 1827.

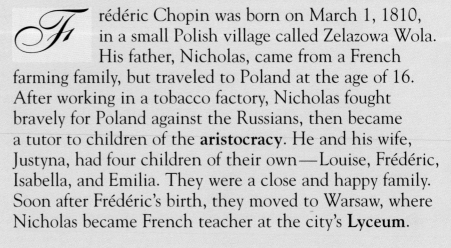

POLAND AT THE TIME OF CHOPIN'S BIRTH

At the end of the eighteenth century, Poland was surrounded by three great empires—Prussia, Austria, and Russia. All three wanted to increase their power, and Poland suffered the consequences of their political deals. The country was divided up in 1772 and again in 1773. This sparked the uprising in which Chopin's father took part. Russian troops put down the rebellion, and Poland was divided up yet again in 1795. This Third **Partition** gave Warsaw—the city where Chopin grew up—to Prussia. But in 1807 the French Emperor, **Napoleon**, invaded Prussia and turned Warsaw into a **Grand Duchy**, with its own king. After Napoleon's defeat in Russia in 1812, Warsaw fell into Russian hands. The **Czar** of Russia, Alexander I, became ruler of the Grand Duchy and King of Poland. His harsh rule made people angry, so secret societies were created that plotted to throw the Russians out of Poland.

Czar Alexander I (1777–1825) led Russia through many wars against Napoleon and helped to bring peace in Europe.

At a very early age, Frédéric began to experiment on the piano, and his parents soon realized that he had a strong feeling for music. When he was seven, they arranged for him to have piano lessons with Adalbert Zywny, an elderly composer. Zywny played the violin well but was not really a pianist, so Frédéric taught himself to play. But he did receive a basic musical education from Zywny and learned to appreciate the masters— **Bach, Mozart,** and **Beethoven**. He also enjoyed **improvising** at the keyboard. While still only seven, he turned one of his improvisations into a proper piece, which was then published. The next year he performed publicly as a pianist for the first time, at a charity concert. From then on, when not at school, he was always playing and composing. He soon became well-known in Warsaw as a musical prodigy.

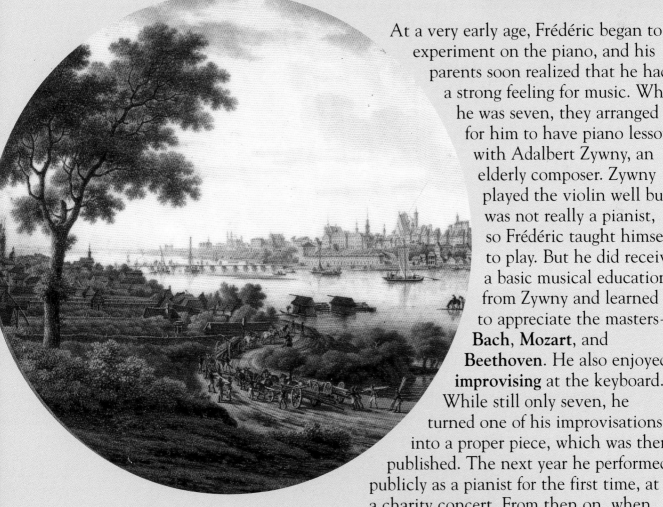

The city of Warsaw around the time of Frédéric's childhood. The city was built beside the Vistula River, in the middle of open plains.

POLAND'S YOUNG GENIUS

Frédéric Chopin as a teenager. He was an unusually sensitive young man and had a sharp sense of humor.

W hile still a teenager, Frédéric was often invited to play in the houses of Warsaw's aristocrats. These drawing-room, or **salon**, concerts were very popular in grand society during the early nineteenth century. They became the main part of Frédéric's performing career, and it was here that he began to **improvise** versions of Polish dances, such as the mazurka and the polonaise. Frédéric mixed well with wealthy people. His elegant manners and looks made him seem a perfect gentleman. People said he had the charm of a prince.

In 1825, Frédéric was asked to play for Warsaw's ruler, Alexander I, the Czar of Russia. Alexander was so impressed that he gave the fifteen-year-old a diamond ring. The next year Frédéric **enrolled** at Warsaw's **Conservatory** of Music to learn traditional **music theory**. But he rebelled against old-fashioned rules of composition, preferring to invent his own kind of music.

The Conservatory of Music in Warsaw is the building between the two towers on the left of this picture. It was founded by Chopin's teacher, Josef Elsner.

POLONAISES AND MAZURKAS

The polonaise and the mazurka are forms of traditional Polish dances. The same names are given to pieces of music written to accompany them. Each dance has its own special rhythm and style. The polonaise is stately and grand. Chopin would have danced it often at the aristocratic balls he attended in Warsaw. The mazurka, by contrast, is a traditional dance of country people. It is much simpler, and the accompanying music often has a beautiful, haunting tune. Chopin particularly enjoyed spending time on the country estates of his school friends, and it was during these holidays that he became familiar with the mazurka.

Chopin's piano compositions were enormously influenced by these two dance forms. He developed many different ways of presenting them, usually by laying beautiful, song-like melodies over the top of their basic rhythms. As the years went by, his polonaises and mazurkas became a way for him to express his deep love and longing for Poland. Instead of simply being dance music, they became intensely patriotic musical poems.

The great Italian violinist Niccolò Paganini (1782–1840) wrote such difficult music for the violin that only he himself was able to play it at the time.

By this time, Frédéric was keen to travel abroad because he thought Warsaw did not offer him enough musical opportunities. Occasional visits from famous **virtuosos**, such as the violinist Paganini and the pianist **Hummel**, gave him glimpses of a world of music beyond Poland. In 1828, Frédéric accompanied a friend of his father's on a short trip to Berlin. He enjoyed the experience so much that he decided to leave Warsaw as soon as his studies were complete.

Frédéric's teacher, Josef Elsner, did not approve of his student's waywardness. But he was wise enough to recognize that Chopin was a genius, and so did not interfere.

Elsner was proved right in 1827, when Frédéric composed a remarkable new work. It was a set of piano **variations** based on a tune called *Là ci darem*, which is a love duet from an **opera** by Mozart. The work showed that Frédéric could express himself in music like a poet and understood how to get the best effects from a piano.

Chopin plays the piano in the elegant salon of his friend Prince Anton Radziwill.

9

TRIUMPH IN VIENNA

The Kärntnerthor Theater, where Chopin made his first public appearance in Vienna, on August 11, 1829.

Vienna in the early nineteenth century was one of the most important musical centers in Europe. It had been home to the three greatest composers in living memory—Mozart, **Haydn**, and Beethoven—and was full of rich **patrons** and brilliant performers. After finishing at the Warsaw Conservatory in July 1829, Frédéric set off on vacation to Vienna, taking with him dazzling letters of introduction from his teacher, Elsner. He could not have hoped for a more exciting welcome. News about his genius had spread fast, and suddenly all of Vienna wanted to hear him play.

A music publisher called Haslinger offered to publish the *Là ci darem* variations, on condition that Frédéric play them at two concerts. He was a little nervous about performing, but finally agreed to the concerts when he heard that one of the best theaters in the city had been reserved specially for him.

Virtuoso composers were all the rage at the time, and Frédéric's concerts caused a sensation, particularly the brilliant improvising. However, some people commented that his playing was a little softer than they were used to.

In September 1829, Frédéric returned to Warsaw, delighted with his triumph. Then he began his most important work to date, Piano **Concerto** in F minor. It was also at this time that he fell madly in love with a beautiful young singer called Constantia Gladkowska. He was too shy to tell her, but managed instead to express his affection in the piano concerto's slow **movement**.

Much as he loved Poland, his family, and Constantia, Frédéric now decided that the time had come to follow up his earlier triumph in Vienna. He also hoped to travel elsewhere in Europe and to find a great teacher to help him perfect his playing. Frédéric left Warsaw for Vienna on November 2, 1830. He was never to return. His former teacher, Elsner, composed a song of farewell and arranged for a small choir to sing it as Frédéric waved goodbye.

Ludwig van Beethoven (1770–1827) revolutionized music in Vienna, but died two years before Chopin's arrival.

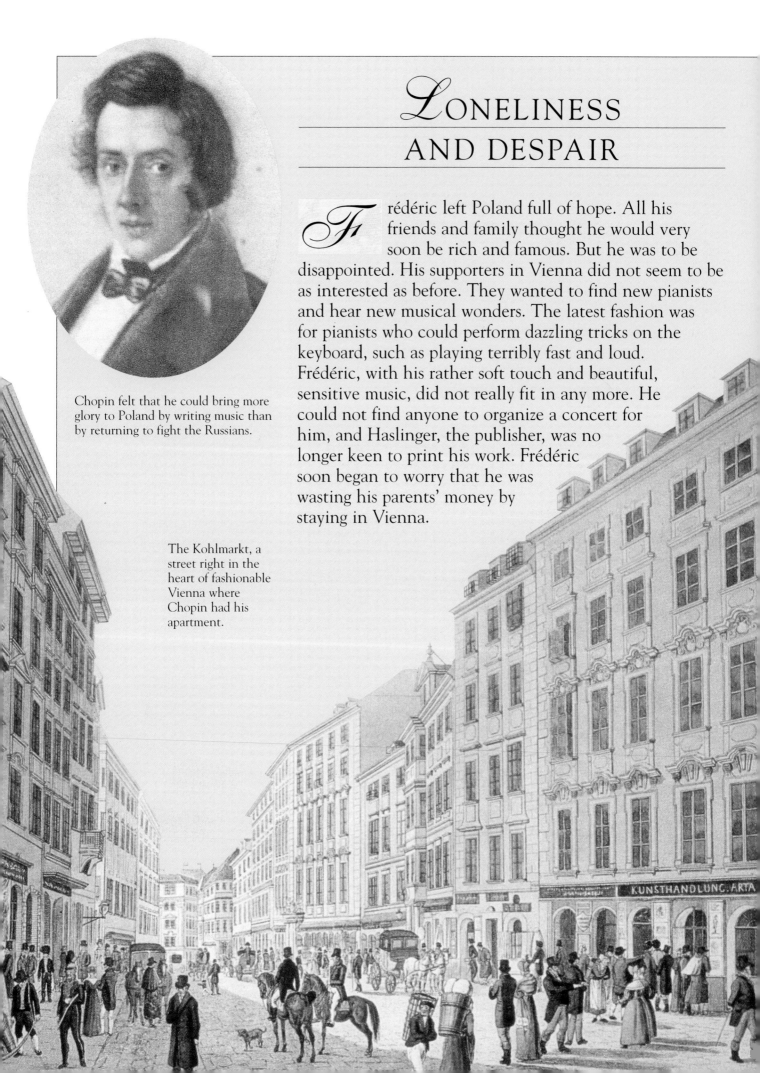

LONELINESS AND DESPAIR

Chopin felt that he could bring more glory to Poland by writing music than by returning to fight the Russians.

Frédéric left Poland full of hope. All his friends and family thought he would very soon be rich and famous. But he was to be disappointed. His supporters in Vienna did not seem to be as interested as before. They wanted to find new pianists and hear new musical wonders. The latest fashion was for pianists who could perform dazzling tricks on the keyboard, such as playing terribly fast and loud. Frédéric, with his rather soft touch and beautiful, sensitive music, did not really fit in any more. He could not find anyone to organize a concert for him, and Haslinger, the publisher, was no longer keen to print his work. Frédéric soon began to worry that he was wasting his parents' money by staying in Vienna.

The Kohlmarkt, a street right in the heart of fashionable Vienna where Chopin had his apartment.

A Viennese musical evening. The composer Schubert plays to a group of admiring friends.

Frédéric's social life was busy. He had a fine apartment in the center of town, and often went to parties. But his fun was ruined by news from Poland. Warsaw had revolted against Russia, and the Czar had sent an army of 120,000 men into the city.

Frédéric had nightmares about the Russian revenge. He imagined his friends and family being murdered, but was powerless to help them. He felt lonely and desperate. His compositions of the period, such as the *Revolutionary* **Study** in C minor and the **Scherzo** in B minor, express this inner struggle. They are energetic, restless and angry pieces of music.

Frédéric began to despise Viennese musical taste and wondered if he should leave the city. The failure of two concerts he gave in the spring of 1831 helped him make up his mind. He left Vienna in July without regret, and set out for Paris, the heart of music in Europe. On the way, he stopped in Germany, where he received a devastating piece of news. Warsaw had fallen to the Russians. Frédéric was in complete despair and his imagination ran wild. He feared the worst for his family.

THE POLISH UPRISING OF 1830

1830 was a year of rebellions in Europe. They were sparked off by a revolution in France in July 1830, when students and workers rose up in Paris to overthrow the king, Charles X. A new king, Louis Philippe, was crowned in his place. News of this revolution spread across Europe, where secret societies in other countries plotted their own uprisings. The Poles rose up against the Russian Czar on November 29, 1830. By January 1831, they had declared that he was no longer King of Poland. This led to a full-scale war.

No other European countries came to Poland's rescue because they did not dare to risk conflict with Russia. The rebellion was finally put down by the vast Russian army in September 1831. Poland was then swallowed up into the Russian Empire.

The Polish army, broken and defeated, gives up its struggle against the might of Russia.

CHOPIN SETTLES IN PARIS

Paris was a new and thrilling experience for Frédéric. The streets teemed with life and excitement. It was only a year since the 1830 revolution, and people still felt full of hope for the future. Shouts of "Liberty!" were often heard in the city, as was the great revolutionary anthem, the "Marseillaise." Paris was also home to an extraordinary collection of great artists, writers, and musicians, who often met to exchange new ideas. Soon after arriving, Frédéric was invited to join this group. He got to know the most distinguished musicians in Paris, including the Italian opera composer Rossini, whom he had always admired. The song-like quality of Chopin's piano music owes a lot to the influence of Italian opera.

The great cathedral of Notre Dame looms high above the busy streets of nineteenth-century Paris.

Gioacchino Rossini (1792–1868) was one of the most senior and respected musical figures in Paris. Yet after 1829, he hardly composed at all.

Frédéric now thought that the time had come to perfect his piano playing and planned to study with the pianist **Kalkbrenner**. However, his family persuaded him to start his career as a professional concert pianist instead.

Frédéric's first concert took place in February 1832. The hall was full of well-known musicians, and he was much admired. But at the next concert, in May, the audience began to criticize his playing. They liked the wide range of feelings he was able to express in his music. But like the public in Vienna, they thought his playing was just a little too soft and delicate. This upset Frédéric tremendously.

ARTISTIC LIFE IN PARIS

Chopin immediately felt at home in Paris because there were so many Polish refugees in the city. Refugees from other parts of Europe also fled there, because it was a city in which people were allowed to talk openly about freedom. By 1831, France had been through two revolutions (1789 and 1830), and Paris had become a center for people who valued free speech and new ideas.

Some of the brightest new ideas of the time came from the artists, writers, and musicians who lived in Paris. They formed a close group of friends and often met in one another's houses to discuss their political and artistic views. Among them were French **novelist** Honoré de Balzac and French poet Victor Hugo, who also wrote novels, including *Les Misérables*. The painter Eugène Delacroix was also part of this circle, and he became one of Chopin's closest friends. Other musicians in the group included the brilliant young German composer **Mendelssohn**, the French composer **Berlioz**, and the most popular virtuoso pianist of the day, the Hungarian composer Franz Liszt.

Victor Hugo (1802–1885) was a writer and republican whose opinions affected political feelings in France.

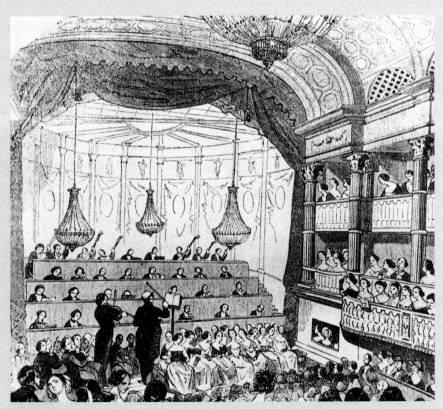

The concert hall of the Paris Conservatory, where Chopin performed.

Chopin now had to decide whether he wanted to be a virtuoso or a composer. He was shy of public concerts, preferring to play at smaller salon **recitals**. But it was difficult to earn a living from these. Just as he was running short of money, he was introduced to one of the world's richest families, the Rothschilds. Frédéric soon became a close friend, and met other wealthy aristocrats. Before long he was a member of Paris **high society** and was offered a number of well-paid teaching posts. At last he was making money.

A
DISAPPOINTED
LOVER

hopin was by now a fashionable person in the music world of Paris. The public grew interested in his compositions, and suddenly several publishers were keen to print his work. Two sets of **nocturnes** and mazurkas were published, followed in 1833 by a first set of piano studies. These consisted of 12 showpieces, each designed to help piano students practice a different technical skill. They are also some of the most beautifully expressive pieces Chopin ever wrote. He composed a second set of 12 shortly after completing the first.

An example of Chopin's musical handwriting. This is the manuscript of a polonaise.

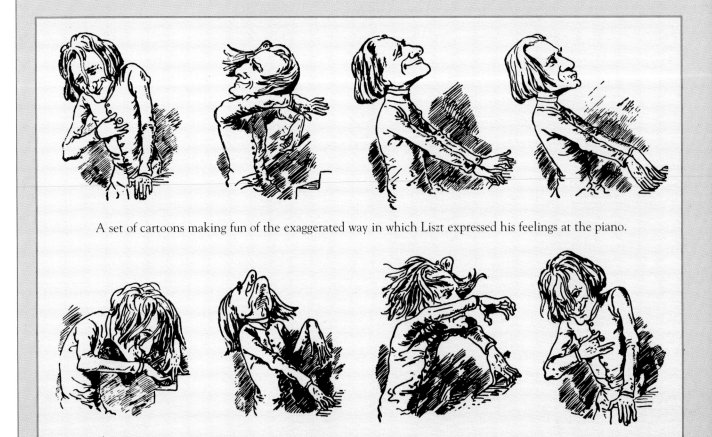

A set of cartoons making fun of the exaggerated way in which Liszt expressed his feelings at the piano.

Franz Liszt, Virtuoso Composer

By 1830 the piano was a very popular instrument. More and more people, especially women, were learning how to play. The greatest musical heroes of the day were virtuoso pianists, and the most glamorous of them all was Franz Liszt (1811–1886). He was handsome, talented, and a great showman. He could play difficult music at great speed and improvise brilliantly. Women, in particular, worshiped him. His performances seemed to cast a magic spell over his audiences. There were even rumors that he was possessed by the devil. He was like a modern pop star—the most fashionable musician of his day.

Chopin was not strong enough to compete with Liszt's energetic style of performance. The two musicians were friends, and Chopin admired Liszt's playing but was annoyed at the public's musical taste. They preferred seeing a flashy show to hearing serious music. Chopin thought that Liszt's own compositions were musically empty—just showpieces.

Liszt was respected as a musician well into old age. His daughter married the German composer Richard Wagner.

Frédéric performed two concerts in 1835, and on both occasions it was clear that the public did not really enjoy his style of playing. They preferred the more spectacular style of superstars like Liszt. Frédéric therefore decided to give up public concerts so that he could concentrate on composing.

By this time, Chopin was earning plenty of money and living comfortably. He felt happy in Paris and did not miss Poland as much as he had at first. But he did long to see his parents again and in August 1835 arranged to meet them in the **Bohemian** town of Karlsbad. It was a very happy reunion, the first since Frédéric had left Poland. Sadly, they were never to meet again. After Karlsbad, Frédéric traveled to Dresden, where he met again with the Wodzinski family, old friends from his early years in Warsaw.

He found that the Wodzinskis' young daughter, Maria, had grown into a beautiful 16-year-old. She was also a talented pianist, and he soon fell in love with her. Maria's parents were fond of Frédéric but were concerned that he was so often ill. When he asked Maria to marry him, in September 1836, they said that the wedding could take place only if he remained healthy. But the following winter Frédéric was ill with flu, and Maria's parents decided that the marriage could not go ahead. Frédéric grew depressed and eventually gave up hope. He wrapped up all his letters from Maria and wrote two words on the package: "my misery."

GEORGE SAND

oward the end of 1836, Chopin went to a party and met a most unusual woman. She was a popular novelist whose name was Aurore Dudevant, although she preferred to be called George Sand.

To begin with, Chopin did not much like George. He was not used to her unconventional behavior, such as dressing in men's clothes and smoking cigars. He was also cautious because of her reputation. She was separated from her husband and lived a free life in Paris, with many lovers. But as he got to know George, and as his hopes of marrying Maria began to fade away, Chopin grew increasingly fascinated by her. He particularly admired her strong, independent personality.

George Sand (1804–1876) was married to Baron Dudevant for nine years, but left him in 1831 to become a writer.

The ship on which Chopin and George Sand traveled to Majorca. It is seen here steaming into the island's main port, Palma.

By the summer of 1838, Frédéric and George were in love and wanted to be together. They decided to leave Paris to avoid creating a scandal and traveled to the island of Majorca, off the coast of Spain. George's two children—Maurice, aged 15, and Solange, aged 8—went, too.

At that time, Majorca was a beautiful, remote place, rarely visited by tourists. The islanders lived a simple life of farming and winemaking. Frédéric and George rented a villa and relaxed blissfully in the warm weather. He started composing, and she writing. "I am really beginning to live," Frédéric wrote to a friend. He felt more healthy than ever before and began to enjoy walking in the countryside. But the paradise did not last. In November, Frédéric caught a severe chill on the way back from a long walk and soon became seriously ill with **bronchitis**.

Majorca in the height of summer. It has become a favorite vacation spot because of its beauty, its mild and fairly dry climate, and its historic interest.

Winter arrived and it began to rain hard. The villa became cold and miserable. A rumor spread that Chopin was dying of consumption. When his landlord heard this, he began to fear that the villa would be infected and ordered Frédéric out. The lovers' dream had become a nightmare.

Chopin (in the center of the room at the back) arriving at the gathering of Paris artists where he meet the novelist George Sand (seated on the left).

A ROMANTIC MONASTERY

Chopin, George Sand, and the two children moved on to a place called Valldemosa, which they had discovered on a walk earlier in the year. It was an old monastery perched high up in the hills, above terraces of vines and fruit trees. The last monks had left long before, and the monastery was empty.

Valldemosa seemed to be the perfect place for two artistic people—lonely, ancient, and surrounded by mountain scenery. But the winter made life very uncomfortable once more. The heavy rain seemed to go on forever, and they could never go out because of winds and mist. Chopin grew more sick and did not like to be left alone. The ghostly sound of wind whistling or bells ringing filled him with terror.

The Abbey Under Oak Trees, by the German painter Caspar David Friedrich, shows the typical Romantic fascination with gloom and fear. It is like a horror-film set.

There were other problems as well. The inhabitants of Majorca, unused to visitors, became hostile. They did not understand why the newcomers, who never went to church, wanted to live in a monastery. George even had difficulty buying food from them, so Frédéric was not receiving enough nourishment to help him recover.

Despite his illness, Chopin composed a little. His piano arrived from Paris in January 1839, and he quickly completed his set of 24 preludes. There is one prelude for each **key signature**, and all are full of melancholy atmosphere. It is easy to imagine Chopin composing them in the lonely monastery, uncertain of his health or future. In February, George realized that Frédéric's life was in danger and arranged to leave Majorca. Their romantic adventure was at an end.

The monastery of Valldemosa in Majorca. This drawing was one of several made by George Sand herself.

ROMANTICISM

Chopin and Sand were
Romantics, members of an
artistic movement known as
Romanticism, which was
popular in the first half of
the nineteenth century.
Romanticism began as a kind
of artistic revolution. Writers,
painters, and musicians
turned away from accepted
ideas about religion, science,
and morals. Instead, they
began to express themselves
freely as individuals, and liked
to cut themselves off from the
world to concentrate on their
own thoughts and feelings.

For their inspiration,
Romantics looked to the
mystery of nature and often
wrote about the uncertainties
of life, such as peculiar twists
of fate, sudden changes in
the weather, or surprising turns of events.
Horror stories and supernatural powers
were also favorite subjects. Chopin's stay
at Valldemosa Monastery was a typical
Romantic adventure: lonely, spooky, wild,
and uncertain. Another important result
of the Romantic movement in music was
the development of virtuoso performers.
The fashion for individual expression
made solo instrumentalists popular.
These musicians seemed to be completely
wrapped up in their own powerful feelings.

On the journey back to
France, Chopin had a
hemorrhage in his lung
and started to cough blood.
But George looked after
him carefully, and soon
after their arrival in the
town of Marseilles, on the
French coast, he began to
recover. They stayed there
for 11 weeks, until Frédéric
felt well enough to plan
his return to Paris.

A nineteenth-century photograph of the house and garden at Nohant. George Sand had inherited the house from her grandmother.

CITY WINTERS, COUNTRY SUMMERS

Louis Philippe (1773–1850) was made king of France after the 1830 Revolution. He was forced to escape to England after the 1848 Revolution, when he was replaced by Prince Louis Napoleon, who later became Napoleon III.

When Chopin felt healthy enough to travel, he and George set off toward Paris. They stopped on the way at George's beautiful country estate, Nohant, 180 miles south of the capital. George had grown up there and never lost her love of country life. They decided to stay for the summer so that Frédéric could recover. Refreshed and happy, he began to compose again, working on his most ambitious project yet. This was Piano **Sonata** in B flat minor. The slow movement is famous for its Funeral March.

As autumn approached, Chopin grew keen to return to Paris. He missed his Polish friends and the aristocratic salons where he was so popular. He also wanted to renew his contacts with music publishers. The return was planned for October. Frédéric arranged separate addresses for himself and George, to prevent gossip. But the two apartments were so close that they were able to spend every evening together as a family. Frédéric had grown especially fond of George's headstrong daughter, Solange.

For the next few years, Frédéric and George spent their winters in Paris and their summers in the country at Nohant. Life in Paris was a whirlwind of parties and musical evenings. Frédéric often ended up entertaining his friends by improvising at the piano long into the night. But during the summer he relaxed and devoted himself to composing. Close friends, such as the opera singer **Pauline Viardot** and the painter Eugène Delacroix, often came to stay for weeks on end.

Despite his fear of public concerts, Chopin was persuaded to perform twice, in 1841 and 1842. He also played for the king, Louis Philippe, at the Tuileries Palace, for which he was given a fine set of porcelain. Chopin did not enjoy the strain of these performances, however, and still preferred to earn his living by teaching.

EUGÈNE DELACROIX (1798–1863)

Eugène Delacroix was the most important and influential painter in France during Chopin's lifetime. He was also one of the leaders of the Romantic movement.

Delacroix's huge paintings were dramatic and powerful. He used bright colors, strong lighting effects, and free brushwork to bring his subjects to life. Although he often painted scenes from history or myths, the people in his pictures, and their emotions, seem very real. This was because Delacroix used his paintings to express his own feelings about life, in a typically Romantic way. For example, he was obsessed with the idea of violent death and often returned to this theme in his work. His style of painting was very unusual at the time, but it greatly influenced the future history of art.

Delacroix was a close friend of Chopin and a regular guest at Nohant in the summer. George Sand even had one of her stables specially converted into a studio for him.

The Lion Hunt, painted by Eugène Delacroix. It is typical of the artist's work, full of energy, violence, and action.

MOODS
AND
QUARRELS

A portrait of Chopin, by his friend Eugène Delacroix.

Chopin worked hard during his peaceful summers in the country at Nohant. He was given the most beautiful room in the house and composed many pieces of music. But there was a change in his style. He became much more ambitious, wanting to write longer, more complicated works.

The dining room at Nohant, looking out to the garden. Nohant today looks much the same as it did when George Sand and Chopin were alive.

Chopin sent for textbooks about the art of composing and explored adventurous new ways of expressing himself. As time went by, he became too much of a perfectionist and never felt quite satisfied with his work. This began to tire him out. He had never properly recovered from his illness, and now grew moody as well.

Some of Chopin's most brilliant and passionate works, such as the third and fourth **ballades** and the Polonaise in A flat, were composed during these years. Perhaps the greatest triumph was his Third Piano Sonata in B minor, which was written in 1844. Chopin was able to use the keyboard to produce a huge range of musical effects. He was the first composer to understand the piano so perfectly. He rarely wrote for any other instrument but did compose a beautiful cello sonata in 1847 for his friend, the cellist Auguste Franchomme.

By this time, Chopin's relationship with George Sand was under strain. She had begun to treat him like a frail son—perhaps because she so often took care of him. As a result, Frédéric started to imagine she had other lovers and grew jealous. They also disagreed about politics. George was a **democrat** and believed in the rights of ordinary people. Frédéric believed in the power of aristocrats, kings, and the Roman Catholic Church. In 1847 they had a dreadful quarrel. George's son, Maurice, sided with his mother against Frédéric and Solange. After more misunderstandings, Frédéric and George decided not to see each other again. Their long relationship was over.

George Sand's daughter, Solange, shared her mother's willful character. She remained close to Chopin after his relationship with George had come to an unhappy end.

France suffered a bad harvest in 1846, and as a result, ordinary people were short of food. Food riots were encouraged by revolutionaries in an attempt to bring down the government.

$\mathscr{S}$ICK AT HEART

$\mathscr{C}$hopin composed very little music in 1847. He felt depressed after his quarrel with George Sand, and was no longer able to spend the summer relaxing at Nohant. Life in Paris exhausted him, and by the beginning of 1848, he was seriously weak again. He agreed to give a public concert in February, even though he felt that he could no longer play well. It was to be his last concert in Paris.

Revolutions had begun to spread across Europe again, and in February there was an uprising in Paris. Fighting broke out in the streets, and musical life in the city came to a standstill. Chopin's world of salon recitals and elegant parties was finished. As a result, he decided to leave France for a while, accepting the invitation of a pupil called Jane Stirling to visit England. By the end of April, he was settled in a luxurious apartment in the center of London.

London in the nineteenth century, much as Chopin would have known it. St. Paul's Cathedral can be seen in the distance.

Queen Victoria and Prince Albert were a devoted couple, and they had nine children. Albert died in 1861, and the Queen had a nervous breakdown.

The English aristocracy took Chopin to its heart. Everybody wanted to meet him and hear him play, including Queen Victoria and her husband, Prince Albert. Chopin often appeared at drawing-room concerts, and took on several wealthy pupils. These jobs helped pay his bills, but tired him out.

THE REVOLUTION OF 1848

During the 1840s many of France's leading writers and thinkers, including Victor Hugo and George Sand, became interested in **socialism**. This led them to speak up for the rights of ordinary men and women. Workers in cities were influenced by socialism, too. They were angry at the dishonesty of King Louis Philippe's government and held meetings to discuss ways of changing the political system.

In 1846 a bad harvest led to a desperate shortage of food, and France was faced with a crisis. Businesses collapsed, and huge numbers of people lost their jobs. On February 22, 1848, thousands of workers and students came out onto the streets of Paris and clashed with police. The king was forced to choose between civil war and abdication. He fled across the Channel to England, and France was declared a republic. But only four years later, in 1852, the republic collapsed when the country's president, Louis Napoleon Bonaparte, was made emperor.

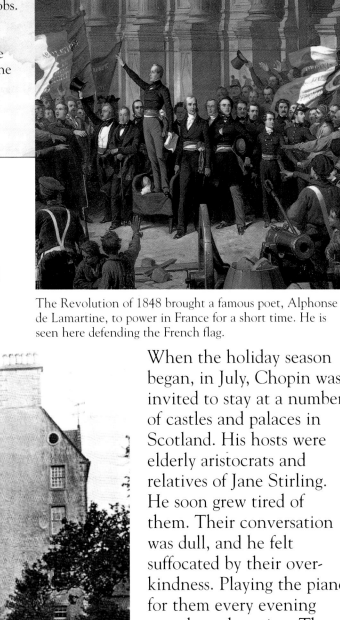

The Revolution of 1848 brought a famous poet, Alphonse de Lamartine, to power in France for a short time. He is seen here defending the French flag.

Soon despite all the popularity and the fans, Chopin felt sick at heart. The London **smog** depressed him, and his cough was getting worse. Jane Stirling looked after him as well as she could and made sure he had whatever he needed. She was probably in love with him.

An old photograph of Calder House, Scotland, where Chopin stayed in 1848.

When the holiday season began, in July, Chopin was invited to stay at a number of castles and palaces in Scotland. His hosts were elderly aristocrats and relatives of Jane Stirling. He soon grew tired of them. Their conversation was dull, and he felt suffocated by their over-kindness. Playing the piano for them every evening was also exhausting. The situation was made more difficult as Chopin did not speak a word of English.

27

An Incurable Illness

Chopin returned to London from Scotland in October 1848. He felt terribly ill and longed to return to his friends in Paris. London's gray weather and smog made him even more gloomy. On November 16 he gave his last public concert. It was a charity event, held at London's **Guildhall** to raise money for Polish refugees. Chopin had so little strength that he was able to play for only an hour.

Chopin, shortly before his death. By this time he was extremely ill and hardly had the strength to compose.

Chopin's last concert was a ghastly struggle for him. He could hardly wait to leave the Guildhall, London, and England.

A week later Chopin returned to Paris, where his friends were deeply concerned about how ill he had become. Doctors were called in, but there was very little they could do. He was suffering from consumption, which at that time was an incurable illness. There was soon another problem to face—a shortage of money. Chopin had been feeling too downhearted to compose and had published nothing for nearly two years. Luckily, rich friends such as the Rothschilds came to his rescue again with gifts of money. Jane Stirling also sent a large sum anonymously.

Chopin knew he was dying. His friends, especially the painter Delacroix and George Sand's daughter, Solange, came to visit and cheer him up. But his greatest wish was to see his family, so he wrote to his sister Louise, begging her to visit.

Chopin's body is buried in this grave, at the Père Lachaise Cemetery, in Paris. But his heart is in a church in Warsaw.

The room in which Chopin died in 1849. On the table are plaster casts of his face and hand.

Louise eventually arrived from Warsaw on August 8, 1849. Day and night she sat by Chopin's bedside, comforting him and talking to him. But no amount of love and care from his sister could defeat the composer's illness. Just over two months later, at two o'clock in the morning on October 17, Chopin finally died. Both Louise and Solange were at his side.

Chopin's funeral was a grand and moving event. It was held at the Church of the Madeleine in Paris, and Mozart's *Requiem* was performed, as Chopin had wished. Large numbers of distinguished aristocrats and artists attended to say a last farewell to their great friend. Chopin's body was buried in Paris, but Louise took his heart in an urn back to Poland, where he was born. There it was placed in Warsaw's Church of the Holy Cross.

TIME CHART

1810	Frédéric Chopin born at Zelazowa Wola, Poland, March 1.
1818	Gives his first concert, aged eight, February 24.
1827	Emilia Chopin dies of consumption. Composes *Là ci darem* variations.
1828	Travels to Berlin, September.
1829	Leaves the Warsaw Conservatory, July. Travels to Vienna, arriving July 31. First concert in Vienna, August 11.
1830	Leaves Warsaw for the last time, November 2. Arrives in Vienna, November 22.
1831	Leaves Vienna, July. End of Polish revolt—Warsaw falls to the Russians, September 8. Arrives in Paris, mid-September.
1833	First set of studies published, July.
1835	Stays with his parents in Karlsbad, summer.
1836	Asks Maria Wodzinska to marry him, September. Meets George Sand.
1838	Arrives in Majorca, November 7.
1839	Leaves Majorca, February 13. Arrives back in Paris, October.
1844	Completes the Third Piano Sonata in B minor, summer.
1847	Separates from George Sand, summer.
1848	Last concert in Paris, February 16. Revolution in Paris, February 22. Arrives in England, April 20. Travels to Scotland, July. Final concert, at the Guildhall, London, November 16. Leaves London for Paris, November 23.
1849	Frédéric Chopin dies in Paris, October 17.

GLOSSARY

aristocracy people who inherit power, money, and property from their ancestors. Members of the aristocracy usually have titles, for example, duke or earl.

Bach, Johann Sebastian (1685–1750) German composer who wrote large-scale, complex church music, as well as instrumental and keyboard works. He was renowned during his life as a brilliant organist.

ballade a word Chopin used to describe some of his long, very dramatic piano works.

Beethoven, Ludwig van (1770–1827) German composer who lived in Vienna, and is often seen as the founder of Romantic music. He was a remarkable pianist and also revolutionized orchestral music.

Berlioz, Hector (1803–1869) French composer of the Romantic movement. He liked to write large-scale works involving huge orchestras and large numbers of singers.

Bohemia a state within the Austrian empire that later became part of Czechoslovakia.

bronchitis a chest illness that brings on heavy coughing.

caricatures cartoons that make fun of people's appearance or behavior.

concerto a piece of music written for orchestra and solo instruments.

conservatory a word used to describe a music college.

consumption a serious infection that attacks the lungs. Before a cure was found, consumption was a killer disease. The modern name for this disease is tuberculosis.

czar the title given to the Russian monarch.

democrat someone who believes that every person in a country should have the right to vote for the government of that country.

enrolled accepted or registered as a member.

Grand Duchy a special word used to describe an independent royal state. The king who ruled the Grand Duchy of Warsaw was, more accurately, the Grand Duke of Warsaw.

Guildhall a grand building in the city of London, used for ceremonial events such as state banquets.

Haydn, Joseph (1732–1809) Austrian composer who was particularly skilled at writing music for orchestras and for groups of four string players, called quartets.

hemorrhage blood escaping through a burst vein.

high society the most wealthy and glamorous people in a country or city.

Hummel, Johann Nepomuk (1778–1837) Hungarian composer who was a pupil of the great Mozart and a child-star pianist. Later in life he became one of the greatest virtuosos in Europe.

improvise compose a piece of music while actually performing it, rather than play it from memory or from written music.

Kalkbrenner, Friedrich Wilhelm (1785–1849) brilliant German pianist and piano teacher who also composed some works for the piano.

key signature one of the "families" into which written music is grouped. Each key signature is known by a letter (A, B, C, D, E, F, or G), together with variations ("sharp," "flat," "major" and "minor"). There are 24 key signatures altogether, and the music sounds higher or lower, depending on which one is used.

Lyceum school or college.

"Marseillaise" revolutionary song composed by an amateur during the French Revolution, in 1792, and later adopted as the French national anthem. The "Marseillaise" was banned by Napoleon and was only used again after the 1830 Revolution. The song was first sung in Paris by people from Marseilles, hence its name.

Mendelssohn, Felix (1809–1847) German composer, brilliant as a child and popular as an adult. He spent much time traveling, and was a favorite of Queen Victoria in England.

movement a piece of music that forms part of a larger composition. A typical sonata or concerto is divided into three or four different movements.

Mozart, Wolfgang Amadeus (1756–1791) Austrian composer, often described as the most brilliant musical genius in history. Although he lived only a short while, he produced vast numbers of works, most of which are masterpieces.

music theory the rules and logic that govern music.

Napoleon (1769–1821) Emperor of France from 1804 to 1814. Born on the island of Corsica, he became a famous general while still young, and began ruling France in 1799. After fighting wars in Europe, he was finally exiled to St. Helena, an island in the Atlantic Ocean.

nocturne a slow piano piece with a clear tune played by the right hand. Originally, a nocturne was a musical piece that expressed the calm of night.

novelist a person who writes novels (books with invented stories).

opera a musical drama in which the performers sing most or all of the lines, usually accompanied by an orchestra. The music is just as important as the words in an opera.

partition the act of dividing up a country.

patrons people who support an artist by providing money or employment.

prelude a piece of music written to be played before other pieces. Chopin's 24 *Preludes*, however, are just individual short piano pieces.

recital a concert with very few performers, or organized to show off the talents of one particular musician.

salon a word used to describe recitals that take place in a small room, or the drawing room of an elegant household.

scherzo an Italian word meaning "joke" that is used to describe individual pieces of music that are lively and full of feeling.

smog a thick, smoky fog that used to be common in London in the days when people in the city had open fires in their homes.

socialism a political movement aimed at trying to create a fairer society, with less of a difference between the rich and the poor.

sonata a piece of music written for the piano or for another instrument accompanied by the piano.

study a type of piano piece that can be used to improve the pianist's playing technique. In a set of studies, each one focuses on a different technical problem.

variations different musical versions of an original tune.

Viardot, Pauline (1821–1910) one of the greatest opera singers of the nineteenth century. She was part of the Garcia family, which produced several other outstanding singers.

virtuoso a particularly skillful performer who has mastered all the techniques of playing a chosen musical instrument.

INDEX

Allº con brio

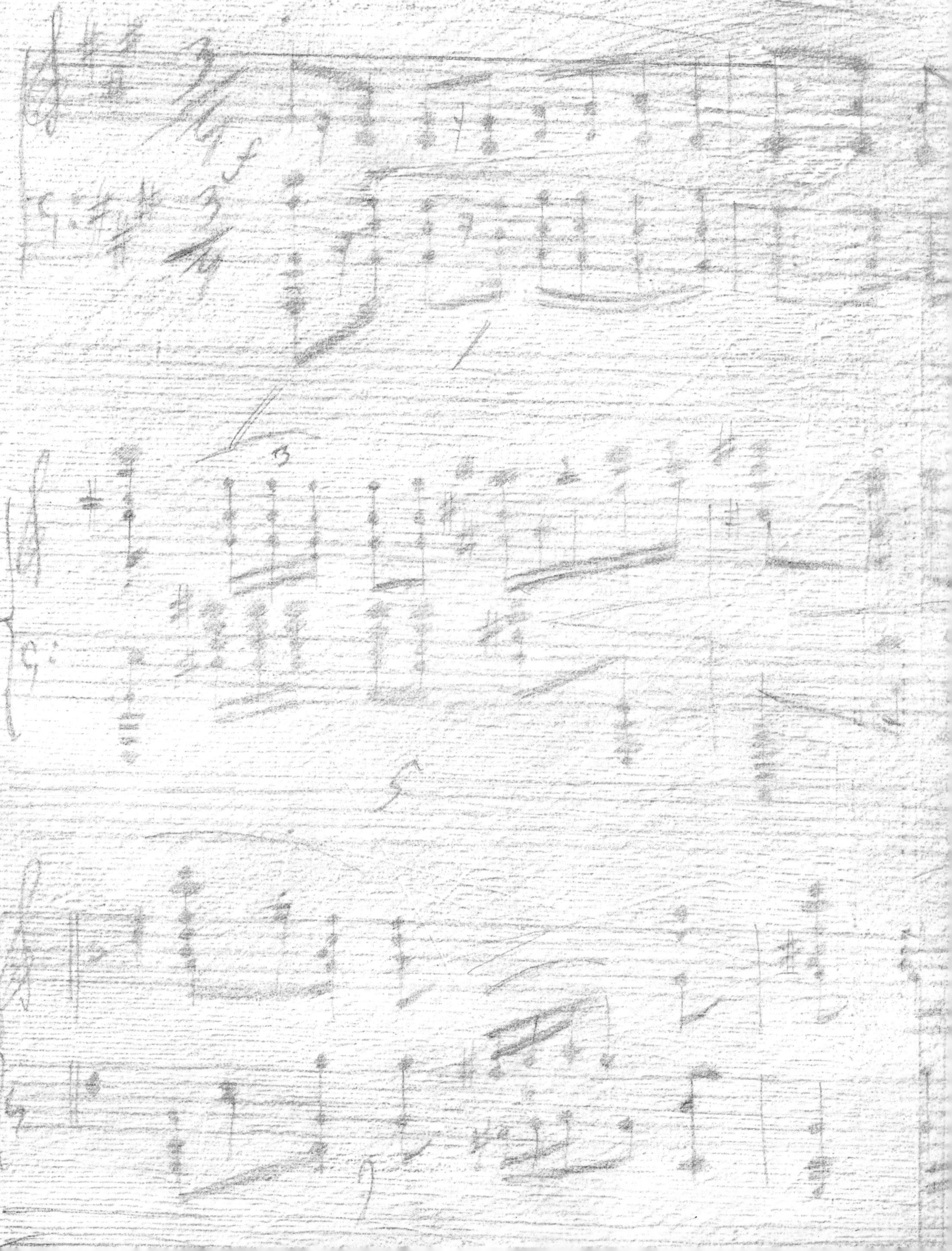